KIDS AROUND the WORLD

Getting All Dressed Up!

By Patty Michaels

Illustrations by Clarice Elliott

Ready-to-Read

SIMON SPOTLIGHT

An imprint of Simon & Schuster Children's Publishing Division • New York Amsterdam/Antwerp London Toronto   Sydney/Melbourne   New Delhi • 1230 Avenue of the Americas, New York, New York 10020 • For more than 100 years, Simon & Schuster has championed authors and the stories they create. By respecting the copyright of an author's intellectual property, you enable Simon & Schuster and the author to continue publishing exceptional books for years to come. We thank you for supporting the author's copyright by purchasing an authorized edition of this book. No amount of this book may be reproduced or stored in any format, nor may it be uploaded to any website, database, language-learning model, or other repository, retrieval, or artificial intelligence system without express permission. All rights reserved. Inquiries may be directed to Simon & Schuster, 1230 Avenue of the Americas, New York, NY 10020 or permissions@simonandschuster.com. • This Simon Spotlight edition January 2026 • Text © 2026 by Simon & Schuster, LLC • Illustrations © 2026 by Clarice Elliott • All rights reserved, including the right of reproduction in whole or in part in any form. SIMON SPOTLIGHT, READY-TO-READ, and colophon are registered trademarks of Simon & Schuster, LLC. For information about special discounts for bulk purchases, please contact Simon & Schuster Special Sales at 1-866-506-1949 or business@simonandschuster.com. Simon & Schuster strongly believes in freedom of expression and stands against censorship in all its forms. For more information, visit BooksBelong.com. The Simon & Schuster Speakers Bureau can bring authors to your live event. For more information or to book an event contact the Simon & Schuster Speakers Bureau at 1-866-248-3049 or visit our website at www.simonspeakers.com. Manufactured in the United States of America 1125 LAK • 2 4 6 8 10 9 7 5 3 1 • CIP data for this book is available from the Library of Congress.
ISBN 9781665983457 (hc) • ISBN 9781665983440 (pbk) • ISBN 9781665983464 (ebook)

Glossary

accessories: items that add to the beauty, convenience, or effectiveness of something else

clans: groups of people who descend from a common ancestor

culture: the shared customs, beliefs, values, and behaviors of a group

flamenco: a traditional dance and music style of southern Spain

garment: item of clothing

identity: the characteristics or personality of a person that sets them apart from others

Indigenous: relating to the earliest people known to live in a place

symbol: something that represents or stands for something else

tribes: social groups made up of people with shared ancestry and language

voyagers: people who travel long distances to another place, often as explorers

Note to readers: Some of these words may have more than one definition. The definitions above match how these words are used in this book.

Contents

Chapter 1:

Always in Style 4

Chapter 2:

Dressed to the Nines 14

Chapter 3:

Hats Off to You! 24

Dress Your Best! 32

Note to readers: Many regions and cultures have unique styles. Here are just some of the special clothing and accessories worn around the world.

Chapter 1:
Always in Style

Clothing and **accessories**
(say: ack-SEH-suh-reez)
can hold special meaning for
many people around the world.

Roll up your sleeves and journey across the globe to explore some of the ways people dress their best!

Many communities around the world have traditional clothes that are important to their **culture** (say: KUHL-chur).

The kimono (say: kee-MOH-noh) is the national **garment** (say: GAR-muhnt) of Japan. The patterns on the fabric can have special meanings.

For example, cranes represent good fortune, and plum blossoms are a **symbol** (say: SIM-bul) of strength.

Another type of clothing with colorful patterns is the dashiki (say: duh-SHEE-kee), which is worn in many West African countries. It is made with lightweight fabric that is suitable for the warm climate.

A kilt is a traditional skirt from Scotland. The plaid patterns are called tartans. Many tartan patterns represent certain Scottish **clans**. The kilt is a symbol of Scottish pride and nationality.

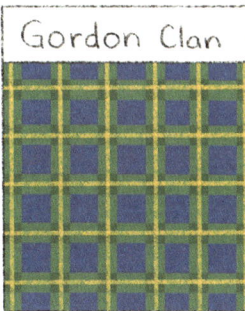

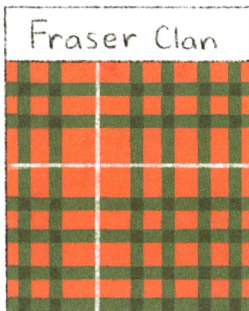

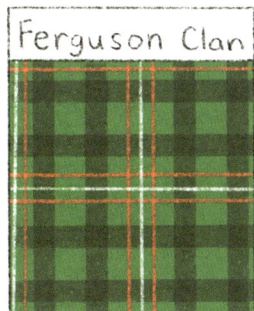

Gordon Clan

Fraser Clan

Ferguson Clan

In India, Pakistan, Bangladesh, and other countries in South Asia, many people wear saris. The sari (say: SAR-ee) is a piece of fabric that can be up to nine yards long. There are over one hundred ways to drape and style a sari!

The gho (say: GOH) and
kira (say: KEE-rah) are the
national garments of Bhutan.
People in Bhutan wear the
gho and kira every day
as a symbol of cultural pride.

Seville, Spain, is known for
flamenco (say: fluh-MENG-koh)
dancing. Many dancers wear
a bata de cola (say: BAH-ta deh
COH-la), which is a long-tailed dress
with ruffles that the dancer flips
and flicks during the performance.

From national garments to special-occasion dresses, traditional clothes are always in style! They are important symbols of culture and **identity** for many people around the world.

Chapter 2:
Dressed to the Nines

Dress to impress with special accessories! Jewelry and other types of accessories can be important items in many cultures.

Jade is a precious stone that
is valuable in many places and
cultures around the world.
It can be used to make jewelry
like pendants and bracelets.

In Chinese culture, jade has many meanings, including purity, good fortune, and wisdom.

Silversmithing is the process of crafting objects from silver, and many **Indigenous** (say: in-DIH-juh-nuss) people in North America have been making silver jewelry since the mid-1800s.

Many Native American silverworks feature symbols and materials that are important to native culture, such as animals, nature, and precious stones like turquoise.

In many Kenyan **tribes**,
beaded jewelry is an important
part of their culture and identity.

Natural materials such as seashells, seeds, bones, clay, stone, and wood can be used to make beaded jewelry. They can be worn as bracelets, necklaces, piercings, headdresses, and more!

Early Polynesian **voyagers**
brought the custom of wearing
leis (say: layz) to the Hawaiian Islands.
Historically, Hawaiians wore leis
as a sign of royalty or wealth.

Leis can be made of flowers, leaves, shells, beads, feathers, seeds, nuts, and sometimes animal bones. Today they are a symbol of welcome, love, and respect and can be worn by anyone.

Chapter 3:
Hats Off to You!

Hats are also important accessories worn as symbols of expression in many cultures around the world.

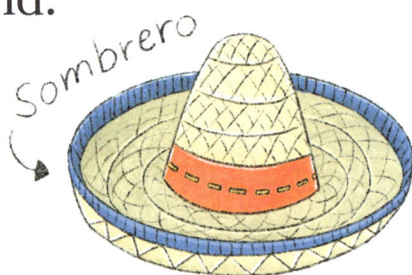

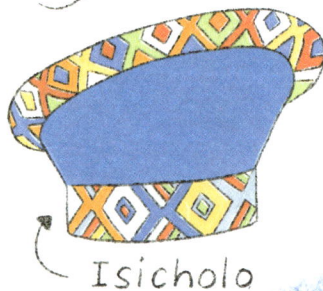

Sombrero

Fedora

Nón Lá

Baseball cap

Beret

Isicholo

In many African communities, hairstyles and headwear can symbolize status. The isicholo (say: ih-see-CHO-low) is a flared hat that is worn by Zulu women in South Africa for special occasions.

The nón lá (say: nawn LAA) is a cone-shaped hat worn in Vietnam. Its unique shape protects the wearer from the sun and rain that is common in the region.

The cone shape is made by sewing palm leaves along a frame of sixteen bamboo hoops.

A sombrero (say: suhm-BRAIR-oh) is a type of hat worn in Mexico, Spain, and the southwestern United States.

The sombrero's wide brim helps the wearer stay cool in these regions' warm environment. The brim can be as wide as two feet!

Now we have seen many
ways people
dress their best!

Clothing and accessories
bring people together to
celebrate unique traditions
and cultures around the world!

Dress Your Best!

Now it's your turn to dress your best! Create your own fashion book that expresses your unique style.

You will need the following:

- **an adult to help you**
- **paper**
- **crayons or markers**
- **a stapler**

Put your thinking cap on and imagine all the clothes and accessories that may be important to you.

- Is there an item of clothing that reminds you of a special memory?

- Do you have something that you wore to an important event?

- Are there meaningful accessories that were gifted to you?

- Does an item symbolize something significant to you?

- Do you have items that have been passed down from family members?

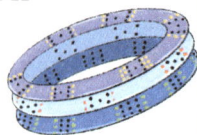

Use paper and crayons or markers to draw your clothing and accessories. Staple the pages together to create your book! Now you have a guide for your unique style!